THE TUDOR REFORMATION

Richard Hayman

First published in Great Britain in 2015 by Shire Publications, part of Bloomsbury Publishing Plc.
PO Box 883, Oxford, OX1 9PL, UK
1385 Broadway, 5th Floor, New York, NY 10018, USA
Email: shire@shirebooks.co.uk   www.shirebooks.co.uk

A CIP catalogue record for this book is available from the British Library.

Shire Library no. 818.   ISBN-13: 978 0 74781 484 9
PDF eBook ISBN: 978 1 78442 070 3
epub ISBN: 978 1 78442 069 7

Richard Hayman has asserted his right under the Copyright, Designs and Patents Act, 1988, to be identified as the author of this book.

Typeset in Garamond Pro and Gill Sans.
Printed in China through World Print Ltd.

17 18 19 20 21   11 10 9 8 7 6 5 4 3 2

COVER IMAGE
Cover design and photography by Peter Ashley, front cover: detail from screen panel in St.Mary's church, Great Snoring, Norfolk. Back cover: Tudor Rose, collection of Peter Ashley.

TITLE PAGE IMAGE
The printed word was crucial to the Reformation. During the reign of Queen Mary, books by the Protestant theologian Martin Bucer were publicly burned, one of the events that fuelled anti-Catholic sentiment in England.

CONTENTS PAGE IMAGE
The priory of St Oswald had a long history, having been built by the River Severn in the Anglo-Saxon period. Its ruins are now stranded in the middle of modern Gloucester.

ACKNOWLEDGEMENTS
Permission to reproduce illustrations has been given by the following:

British Library Board, page 62; Cadbury Research Library, Special Collections, University of Birmingham, title page, pages 6, 10, 11 (bottom), 35, 45 (both), 56 (bottom), 66, 81 (bottom), 84, 87 (top), 88, 89 (all), 90 (all), 91; National Portrait Gallery, pages 39 (top), 47 (both), 48, 49, 50, 51, 65, 68, 69, 81 (top), 83, 86, 87 (bottom), 93; Yale Center for British Art, Paul Mellon Collection, pages 7, 57, 61.

Other photographs are by the author.

Shire Publications is supporting the Woodland Trust, the UK's leading woodland conservation charity, by funding the dedication of trees.

CONTENTS

TRADITION OR SCRIPTURE?

THE REFORMATION WAS the most decisive revolution in English history. During the second and third quarters of the sixteenth century England underwent a profound upheaval that transformed religious experience for everyone. Although people worshipped in the same churches and cathedrals, the churches lost their imagery, colour and candles, and the word of God was no longer heard in Latin but in English. Undoubtedly it was a time of loss, of which the destruction of religious works of art by royal injunction is the most tangible example, but it was also a period of great creativity. The primacy given to the English language had a profound impact on the future direction of English culture, especially its literature. The English landscape was also a changed place. It was littered with abandoned and plundered monasteries, 'bare ruined choirs' that in the long run would stimulate a curiosity about the past that slowly developed into archaeology and heritage as we know them today.

The Reformation spans almost the entire Tudor dynasty, encompassing the reigns of Henry VIII and his three children. Reform began under Henry VIII, but he was a contradictory figure in religious matters. He considered himself Catholic, but his opposition to the Pope ensured that his son and heir was brought up and educated in Protestant ideas. Edward VI succeeded to the throne in 1547 at the age of nine, and the country was governed under a Protectorate. After six years of accelerated reforms Edward fell ill and died before his

Images like this figure of St Michael on the rood screen at Ranworth (Norfolk) are a reminder of the rich visual heritage of the medieval church and its cult of the saints, both of which were curtailed by the Reformation.

FONTANENSE CŒNOBIUM
in agro Eboracensi cella
de Clarevalli fundatum
An Dom. MCXXXII

The Monastery of Fountaynes
in Yorkshire à Cell of
Clarevale Founded in the yeare
of o.r Lord MCXXXII

Authori et Partientali amoris et
honoris ergo hujusce Ecclesiæ
insculptarum curiosi et dono
dant Johannes Healy Ar.

By the seventeenth century monastic ruins had become a symbol of old England. Antiquaries began studying them, and by the eighteenth century it was common to call for their preservation. Fountains Abbey (North Yorkshire) is shown here by William Dugdale, c. 1655.

sixteenth birthday. He was succeeded in 1553 by Mary I, daughter of Henry's first wife, Katherine of Aragon. During her five-year reign she swung the pendulum back in favour of traditional religion before her untimely death from cancer in 1558. The Reformation was put on a more stable long-term footing under Elizabeth I, the daughter of Anne Boleyn, and her long reign of forty-five years undoubtedly helped to settle religious life in England.

The Reformation was a top-down revolution. It was implemented by a small faction of government and senior churchmen and was largely obeyed across the country, but the extent to which people welcomed or resented the changes is very difficult to pin down. There is a consensus among historians that, on the whole, people did not want the Reformation and were slow to accept it. But the historical record is dominated by people at the extremes, the ardent traditionalists and evangelical reformers.

For many people the Reformation was a remarkable spiritual journey. Robert Joseph took his vow as a monk in 1517 and spent the 1530s as abbot of the Benedictine monastery of

Evesham, reciting the daily round of offices in Latin. When the monastery was dissolved in 1540 he was pensioned off, but a year later he accepted reform by becoming a parish priest at the church of All Saints in Evesham, next door to the old abbey, and by 1558 he was the vicar of Cropthorne in Worcestershire, worshipping for the next ten years from the English Book of Common Prayer. For others who lived through it from beginning to end, the Reformation was a traumatic experience. Christopher Trychay, parish priest of Morebath in Devon from 1520 to 1574, lamented the decay of church life and the extent to which reform had wrecked the beauty of the parish church. More than that, it had eroded the structure of village life and drained the parish of its resources, leaving it poorer both spiritually and financially. No wonder some of Trychay's parishioners were among the Western rebels who challenged the reforms in 1549. Other people responded by absenting themselves from church altogether. The Reformation was marked by falling congregations. Some people did not like the reforms, or the counter-reforms of Mary's reign, or were just weary of reform itself. Loyalty to

An Allegory of the Tudor Succession shows all the Reformation monarchs, with Henry VIII in the centre. On the left are Mary I and her husband, Philip II of Spain, and on the right are Edward VI and Elizabeth I.

Rood screens, once out of favour for mystifying the rituals in the chancel, were back in vogue during the nineteenth century, carefully restored and painted. This fine example at Carhampton (Somerset) is now the pride and joy of the church.

parish and the local community was first questioned in these years, when parishioners sought out neighbouring parishes that might conduct their services more to certain tastes or, as Bishop Hooper of Gloucester remarked, where 'he knoweth his faith shall not be examined'.

Other people embraced the reforms, even if they would not live out the reform period. John Foxe documented the execution (or martyrdom) of numerous ordinary citizens, whose open Protestant sympathies became a liability during the five years of Mary's Catholic reign. London was the quickest to embrace reform, exposed as it was to Protestant ideas from mainland Europe, but even here there was strong Catholic support. In 1559, after Mary's death, Catholic mass was celebrated in St Paul's Cathedral and at some of the London parish churches until the last moment that it remained legal. A religious procession in the precinct of the cathedral was disrupted by Protestants, one of whom smashed a cross and carried away the figure of Christ, declaring it the 'Devil's guts'. The Reformation had made England a divided nation.

Knowledge was the root of religious reform and it was used to challenge many of the traditional religious practices of

This rood screen at Kemsing (Kent) was restored in 1894, with new rood figures, reconciling the Church of England with its medieval heritage.

Anti-Catholic feeling was one of the consequences of the Reformation. In an image from John Foxe's *Actes and Monuments* (1563), a visitor absurdly flatters the vanity of the Pope by kissing his feet.

the medieval church. Central to traditional worship was the mass, known in its Protestant form as Holy Communion or the Eucharist. Catholic mass and Protestant Eucharist look similar but the rituals and the priests performing them were quite different. In the Catholic mass worshippers believe the bread and wine are transformed into the body and blood of Christ, known as transubstantiation. Protestants rejected what seemed a quasi-magical rite and replaced it with a simpler commemoration of Christ's Last Supper. Mass was performed by a priest in a ceremony where lay people were spectators. It was the primary role of the parish priest to administer the sacraments such as mass and baptism, rather than to preach, teach or inspire. The priests therefore did not need to be especially articulate or well educated, but needed to be devoted to their role, which was behind the imposition of universal celibacy among the priesthood. By the end of the sixteenth century all that had changed. Priests were now married men and ideally, if not always in practice, were university educated and able to read and expound upon the scripture.

Equally central to traditional religion was purgatory. Purgatory was the spiritual halfway house for those people who were not consigned to hell but needed purging of their earthly sins before they could be admitted to heaven. The mass was said in honour of the dead, in the hope that the living could speed the dead on their way. The mass,

therefore, became the promise of salvation. By the fifteenth century scholars began to question and ultimately to reject the notion of purgatory, because there was no scriptural authority for it. When that happened, the structure of traditional religious life was undermined. The next logical step was that, if tradition was wrong, the only right course for Christians was to study the Bible. This was the essence of debate during the Reformation years. Should Christians follow tradition or be guided solely by scripture?

The mass is depicted on the font at Sloley (Norfolk), with the priest turning to give the blessing. Behind him on the left side is the rope for the sacring bell.

In this sixteenth-century allegory of the Reformation, the authority of scripture is weighed against 'the doctrines and vanities of men's traditions'.

THE OLD CHURCH

THE MEDIEVAL CHURCH was an international institution, the house of God and a miracle of administration. England was part of the Roman Catholic Church, which meant that Christian doctrine and the language of worship were the same from Carlisle to Cadiz to Calabria. It was also subject to a universal law code (canon law) overseen by the Bishop of Rome, the Pope.

The parish was the basic unit of the medieval church. It served the pastoral needs of the lay population and in England had evolved in Anglo-Saxon times. Parish churches came under the oversight of dioceses. In England and Wales these were divided between the ecclesiastical provinces (or archdioceses) of Canterbury, presiding over fourteen English and four Welsh dioceses, and York, presiding over the three northern English dioceses.

Monastic churches were separate institutions, communities of men or women who vowed to live by a prescribed rule of life and conduct, which necessitated living in self-contained communities. In sixteenth-century England there were some ten thousand monks and nuns living in about eight hundred communities, of which about 150 were for nuns. Foundation of medieval monasteries had been especially popular from the tenth to the twelfth centuries, often instigated by kings and noblemen, who were their greatest patrons. Gifts to monasteries included endowments of land, which gave the monks a means to support themselves. There were several

Sinners descend into the jaws of hell on the Wenhaston Doom painting (Suffolk).

monastic orders, depending upon which rule was followed, but the most common were the Benedictine and its reformed version, the Cistercian order. Many of their churches were built in remote places that have since acquired picturesque reputations, such as the Cistercian Fountains Abbey in North Yorkshire, or the Benedictine Lindisfarne Priory off the coast of Northumberland. As landowners, monasteries were responsible for much of the economic development of medieval England.

From the thirteenth century a fresh wave of monasticism became fashionable. This was the friars, who rejected the notion of living apart from the lay populace and set up house in towns and cities, where they busied themselves with pastoral work in the community and became noted as

Continued on three bench-ends at Trent (Dorset) is the Ave Maria (Hail Mary), part of the catechism, and the basis of lay faith.

The sacrament of baptism, as shown on the damaged Seven Sacraments font at Nettlecombe (Somerset).

preachers. The other popular religious institutions of the later Middle Ages were colleges. Some of them, like those of Oxford and Cambridge, were academic, but most were established to pray for the soul of their founders. They were staffed by priests who were subject to a disciplined timetable of daily prayer but, because they had not taken a monastic vow, were known as secular priests. In practice many of these colleges were attached to parish churches, such as Warwick St Mary, which was founded as a college as early as 1123.

For the populace at large, faith was based upon the catechism, that is the Lord's Prayer (or Paternoster), Apostles' Creed and Hail Mary, and the sacraments of baptism, confirmation, matrimony, penance, mass, and extreme unction (anointing the dying). The enduring importance of baptism explains why the oldest of the fixtures in a parish church is usually the font. Penance occurred once a year at Easter, when the priest heard his parishioners' confessions. The other sacraments were experienced only once in a lifetime, with the exception of mass. The mass was the chief sacrament of the medieval church. High mass was performed by the parish priest in the chancel, incorporating the sanctuary where the altar was set up, at the east end of the church. Parishioners did not enter this part of the building. They remained in the nave and aisles and received the consecrated elements usually only once a year, at Easter. For the most part they were observers. The most important stage of the rite was the Elevation of the Host, the moment of transubstantiation at which the bread and wine became the body and blood of Christ.

The Five Wounds, shown here on a bench-end at North Cadbury (Somerset), was one of the most popular symbols of Christ's Passion (that is, the events leading up to his crucifixion).

This image of Pity on the rood screen at Wellingham (Norfolk) shows Christ bearing his wounds, surrounded by symbols of his Passion.

The fifteenth-century bench-ends at Wiggenhall St Germans (Norfolk) depict several of the deadly sins, including gluttony and lust.

In the chancel at Long Melford (Suffolk) is an Easter sepulchre, used before the Reformation for the elaborate rituals during Easter week.

Belief in purgatory made death and memory a central theme in parish-church life. Some remission from the pains of purgatory could be had by obtaining indulgences, pieces of paper issued by bishops and their superiors that granted time off purgatory in exchange for performing or funding specific good works. Indulgences could only reduce purgatory, however, so that the dead needed the prayers of the living, and the living were always conscious that they too would in future need the prayers of others. It had a binding effect on medieval society, and created a supernatural bond between the living and the dead. Wills often bequeathed money for a specified number of requiem masses to be said on behalf of

This screen surrounded the Spring Chapel at Lavenham (Suffolk), established to pray for the soul of Thomas Spring, who died in 1523. The screen incorporates small peepholes, allowing worshippers to kneel and observe the performance of the mass from outside the chantry.

the deceased. The richest members of society could endow chantries especially for this purpose. Chantries were side altars in the parish church, often housed in separate chapels, where the founder paid for the construction of the chapel and altar and for a priest to say mass on his or her behalf for a stipulated length of time, or more often in perpetuity. Less wealthy members of society could subscribe to guilds, which would also say requiem masses at their own altars for their deceased members. The parish church was therefore a place not of one altar, but several.

Medieval religious culture was infused with the cult of the saints. The saints acted as exemplars of lives well lived, and became intercessors between the living and the dead, invoked or prayed to because they were close to God. Carvings of saints were often the object of prayers and devotional candles. Various superstitions also became associated with them. It was believed that whoever looked upon an image of St Christopher would be safe that day from plague or sudden death. For that

Left: In a former chantry chapel at Ashton (Devon) are figures of prophets and the Annunciation on the back of the rood screen and its doors. It shows the elaborate decoration of private chapels in late medieval churches.

Below left: This small but resplendent chantry chapel was built c. 1530 at Evesham St Laurence for Clement Lichfield, the abbot of the town's abbey.

Below right: The end of the rood screen at Bramfield (Suffolk) has blank panels where a side altar once stood, also identifiable by the elaborate piscina in the wall, used for washing the vessels used in the mass.

Left: Images of saints adorned the windows of churches, such as this figure of St Mary Magdalene at Alford (Somerset).

Right: Saints Jude, Matthias and Thomas are among the apostles on the rood screen at Weston Longville (Norfolk).

reason a picture of St Christopher was usually painted on the wall of the church opposite the entrance. Most saints had places associated with them, usually either the place where miracles were performed or where they were martyred. The most famous shrines in England were the shrine of Our Lady of Walsingham in Norfolk, a statue of the Virgin Mary to which miraculous powers were attributed, and the shrine of Thomas Becket in Canterbury Cathedral, the archbishop murdered in 1170 by supporters of Henry II. Great emphasis was placed on tactile representations of the holy, even though there were always critics who saw a cynical trade in false relics. Most monasteries and cathedrals, and many parish churches, had relics, often no more than a bone from a saint, housed in shrines. These were celebrated with processions and masses on the saint's day. Shrines were visited in person or, failing that, people bequeathed money for pilgrimages to be undertaken to these shrines on their behalf.

Opposite: Fourteenth-century stained glass in the church of Eaton Bishop (Herefordshire) features St Michael weighing souls on Judgement Day.

A range of developments increased the complexity of religion in the later Middle Ages, including compulsory rites

At Trull
(Somerset)
bench-ends
of the early
sixteenth century
depict a religious
procession,
including images
of a crucifer and
a priest carrying
a reliquary.

Opposite: The
fifteenth-century
stone pulpit at
Bovey Tracey
(Devon) stands
in front of the
rood screen
and is richly
decorated with
two tiers of
figures.

such as the introduction of penance, and optional ones such as the growing popularity of sermons. Sermons were not a compulsory part of the liturgy, but they grew in popularity initially because of the work of preaching friars. Pulpits appeared in parish churches in the fifteenth century. They were also used for the bidding prayers at the beginning of the mass, where the living and the dead were prayed for, especially the recently deceased and major benefactors to the parish. There are more than two hundred pulpits that survive from the pre-Reformation period. With the introduction of pulpits came pews, often with elaborately decorated ends.

The interiors of medieval churches no longer look as they did in the Middle Ages. Even by the time of the Reformation,

Scenes from scripture were commonly depicted in churches, such as this Annunciation scene on the screen at Loddon (Norfolk), in which the Archangel Gabriel appears before the Virgin Mary.

The rood screen at Ranworth (Norfolk), with altars restored on either side of it, gives a good impression of how such screens appeared before the Reformation.

many churches did not have seating and there were far fewer monuments than they now accommodate. The walls were adorned with images of saints, and sometimes even narrative sequences such as the life of the Virgin Mary. Windows also

had stained-glass figures of saints, and wood or stone carvings of saints were affixed to the walls or arcade piers. By the later Middle Ages the sacred part of the church – the chancel and various chapels – were separated from the secular parts – nave, aisles and porch – by screens. The most significant and the most lavish was the rood screen, which, for parishioners, was the visual focus of the interior. The lower part, or dado, was often decorated with images of apostles or saints. Above the screen was a loft, reached by a stone stair in the nave wall, on which candles were lit, and where actors performed mystery plays. The screen was surmounted, either directly or from a beam above the screen, by an image of Christ (the great 'rood', derived from the Saxon word for cross), flanked by figures of the Virgin Mary and St John the Evangelist. Above the rood, painted on the east wall of the nave, which was usually higher than the chancel, was the Doom, an image of the Day of Judgement. The whole ensemble allowed parishioners to contemplate the Christian universe as they observed the mass.

The Doom painting at Wenhaston (Suffolk), depicting the Day of Judgement, once filled the chancel arch. The shadow of the great rood and figures of Mary and John are clearly visible as blank areas on the painting.

The rood screen at Swimbridge is one of the finest in Devon, testament to the rich lay religious culture in late medieval England.

Country there is evidence of an extremely rich lay religious culture in the late Middle Ages, which can be contrasted with many parts of northern England, where religious resources were far poorer. But, as events from 1536 onwards show, it was not necessarily a reliable guide to religious outlook, as the northern counties would prove more conservative in their religion than, for example, East Anglia. Some of the most

A painted panel at Horsham St Faith (Norfolk) shows a Benedictine monk at the foot of the Virgin Mary, signifying that he was the donor of the work (actually probably a screen, panels from which were later used to make a pulpit).

impressive of Norfolk rood screens were erected on the eve of the Reformation – such as Horsham St Faith in 1528, Wellingham in 1532 and North Burlingham in 1536 – barely a decade before their images of saints were defaced. They show how dramatically religious allegiance could change in a short space of time. Later in the century East Anglia was described as a region of 'most fierce Protestants'.

On the doors of the rood screen at Foxley (Norfolk) are the figures of Saints Jerome and Ambrose, to whom the donors, John Waymont and his wife, beg prayers.

ORIGINS OF THE TUDOR REFORMATION

THE CHURCH'S GREATEST achievement turned out to be one of its greatest problems. A universal church required a bureaucracy to ensure that its doctrines were adhered to uniformly. Church discipline had to be maintained. Bishops organised inspections, or 'visitations', to ensure that parish priests conducted the sacraments in the correct manner with the correct equipment, and that monks and nuns were fulfilling their vows properly. Transgressors against church doctrine were dealt with by ecclesiastical courts. The more serious transgressors were labelled heretics and included theologians and ardent lay people. The church had to contend with secular kings, with whom an uneasy relationship could develop over the jurisdiction of rival ecclesiastical and secular courts, and taxes payable to church or state. This would apply especially to England under Henry VIII. Christianity in Britain was in rude health in the years before the Reformation, but the Reformation arose from criticisms that the church was wrong both in its principles and in its practices.

The quality of the priesthood was a favourite target of reformers by the sixteenth century. John Colet, the Dean of St Paul's Cathedral in London, openly blamed popular ignorance and heresy on the shortcomings of the clergy, whom he lambasted for their laxity, covetous behaviour and worldly ambitions. In this period pluralism was common, whereby a priest held the living of more than one parish, and perhaps also a lucrative post at one of the cathedrals,

On a bench-end at Brent Knoll (Somerset) a bishop is portrayed as a fox preaching to gullible geese, satirising the wealthy and powerful clergy.

leading a comfortable life but leaving pastoral care in the hands of poorly paid and poorly educated curates. Taxes paid to the church in the form of tithes, ostensibly one-tenth of all agricultural produce, were resented, especially those to religious houses that were already conspicuously wealthy. The situation in London was worse. It had an urban economy based on wages and profits, making tithe payments difficult to assess, and so its churches derived much of their income by levying fees for services rendered. Petitions to the crown in 1513 and 1514 complained of excessive charges for marriages and funerals. Things came to a head after 1512 when Richard Hunne, a London merchant, was pursued for the fees relating to his son's burial, which he had refused to pay. In 1514 he was arrested and imprisoned on a charge of heresy, but seven weeks later he was found hanged in his cell. A jury returned a verdict of murder, but the church courts could plead 'benefit of clergy', a status that put the church beyond the reach of the common law. The ecclesiastical court declared its own verdict of suicide, condemned Hunne as a heretic, exhumed his body and burned it. His family forfeited everything, but in the long run the church would receive its comeuppance.

Heresy had not been a large problem in the thirteenth and fourteenth centuries but by the early sixteenth century many people were burned for their beliefs. The most radical early English reformer was John Wyclif (c. 1330–84). He had advocated reading the Bible in English instead of in Latin, and questioned the need for a hierarchical church structure. His numerous followers were known as Lollards, who survived in small numbers into the sixteenth century. Theirs was a more personal religious experience than the community-based traditional religion, and one that rejected the mystical trappings of the church. As activists, Lollards helped in the dissemination of radical literature, including the Bible, especially in London and the south-east. When it came, however, the Reformation was less radical than Wyclif had

advocated two centuries earlier. A new generation of radicals was emerging in the sixteenth century. In 1511 a Coventry heretic rejected the notion of transubstantiation on the basis that God made man and man cannot make God, and that no priest can transform bread just by a form of words. What stoked this new phase of radical thinking in the parishes was the printing press.

It was words and ideas that made the Reformation. 'Faith cometh by hearing and hearing by the word of God' (Romans 10:17) was a favourite quote among radicals of the sixteenth century. Their struggle was to make the Bible the central plank of Christian witness. In 1456 Johann Gutenberg published the first printed edition of the Bible and before long words were made accessible to everyone who had learned to read.

Burning at the stake was the preferred method of execution in late medieval Europe. John Goose was burned as a heretic at Tower Hill, London, in 1473.

The sacrament of extreme unction is depicted on the font at Sloley (Norfolk). Anointing of the dying was based upon tradition and so reformers criticised it for its lack of scriptural authority.

The sacrament of penance is depicted on the font at Sloley (Norfolk). The penitent kneels in front of the priest. On the right, the Devil, in the form of a dragon, is cast out by an angel. Reformers argued that there was no scriptural basis for penance.

William Caxton set up his printing press in London in 1476. Printers needed authors to enable their businesses to prosper, and so many works of radical and orthodox theology were delivered to them.

Another of the consequences of printing was a greater concern for the accuracy of ancient texts that had previously been copied by hand. Study of ancient manuscripts in Hebrew, Greek and Latin spawned the intellectual movement known as Renaissance humanism (not to be confused with the modern form of humanism, which affirms the dignity of life without reference to God). Here were the seeds of reformation. Renaissance humanists brought a new rigour to bear on theology. Scholars began to notice that there was no biblical authority for many of the church's rituals, baptism excepted, and that there was no scriptural authority for the state of purgatory. They exposed many forgeries, including the greatest medieval forgery of them all, the so-called Donation

Helper saints, seen here at Barton Turf (Norfolk), were commonly invoked in the later Middle Ages. St Apollonia, on the left, was invoked by toothache sufferers; St Sitha was invoked by housewives and domestic servants. Reformers came to think of these images as idolatrous.

The pulpit at Trull (Somerset) shows the four doctors of the Roman Church, Saints Gregory, Jerome, Augustine and Ambrose, but since the time of John Wyclif the authority of these figures was questioned by radicals.

of Constantine, the document by which Rome acquired its authority as the mother church of western Christendom.

The most celebrated figure of Renaissance humanism, and a prolific author who kept many printers in business, was the scholar from Rotterdam known usually only by his Christian name, Erasmus (1466 or 1469 to 1536). Erasmus lived a peripatetic life and from 1509 spent five years in England at Cambridge, where he was influential among numerous English theologians. His greatest achievement was the publication in 1516 of the New Testament in Greek, with his own notes and Latin translation. It appeared more than a thousand years after the standard Bible translation, known as the Vulgate, was made, and exposed errors in the earlier translation. Erasmus challenged the position of the Virgin Mary, pointing out that there was no scriptural authority for the assertion that she had remained a virgin all her life. Erasmus was also critical of clerical shortcomings, cynical practices and superstitious errors, but he did not reject the Church of Rome outright, and criticised the doctrine of the German monk Martin Luther. England's foremost Renaissance humanist, Sir Thomas More, the Privy Councillor who advised Henry VIII and who would hold the office of Lord Chancellor, was equally loyal to Rome and critical of Luther.

Martin Luther (1483–1546) was an instrumental figure in the European Reformation. Luther came to reject the notion that a virtuous life was the ladder to heaven. He argued that it was natural to strive for a virtuous life, but that it was God who saves souls, not the people themselves. In other words, we are saved not by our own righteousness, but by Christ's righteousness. Luther developed his doctrine of 'justification by faith', which placed the Crucifixion as the central act of salvation for all those who had faith in it and acted in accordance with that faith. It rendered superfluous much of the medieval liturgy, including purgatory and everything associated with it. The event that marked the beginning of the Reformation, in symbolic if not in actual terms, occurred

Erasmus of Rotterdam (c. 1466–1536), shown in a posthumous engraving by Hieronymus Cock, was the leading humanist scholar of the early sixteenth century and published Latin and Greek editions of the New Testament.

The cult of the Virgin Mary was one of the defining characteristics of medieval Christendom, but reformers considered that it bordered on cult worship. This figure of Mary is at Bale (Norfolk).

Martin Luther, leader of the Reformation in Germany, was the most influential continental reformer in the time of Henry VIII.

in 1517, when Luther pinned to the church door in Wittenberg his ninety-five theses against the trade in papal indulgences, arguing, among other things, that the Pope cannot forgive a person on God's behalf. Luther's text was subsequently printed and was soon in the public domain across Germany. He also wrote a denunciation of the Seven Sacraments, providing the occasion for Henry VIII to write a defence against Luther. Henry's *The Assertion of the Seven Sacraments* was a Europe-wide bestseller, for which he was awarded by the Pope the most ironic of all his titles – Defender of the Faith. This, like other English authors who criticised Luther, including Thomas More, inadvertently made Luther's ideas much better known in England than they had been previously.

Germany reformed from the 1520s under Lutheran guidance, and many of its precepts would later appear in England. Adherents of the reformed churches became known as Protestants. But there were other reformers who would also influence the future Church of England. Martin Bucer (1491–1551) had been a Dominican friar but, influenced by Luther, he left the order and became a significant force in the tolerant city of Strasbourg. He would become a direct influence on the English Reformation when he moved to England in the 1540s. Huldrych Zwingli (1484–1531), based in Zurich, secured reform for much of north-eastern Switzerland. Zwingli went further than Luther by his rejection of transubstantiation. Luther had convinced himself that Christ was mysteriously present in the bread and wine, but Zwingli declared that the bread and wine were simply that and nothing more. As there was no real presence of Christ, the Eucharist became a commemoration of the Last Supper.

MARTINVS   BVCCER

BVCCER·HAT·VIEL·GUTEN·VN·GLERT
ENGELANT·HAT·ER·AVCH·BEKERT
DAR·IST·BEGRABE·NACH·SEIM·ENDT
AVCH·WIDR·AVSGRABEN·VN·VERBRENT
ABER·DIE·KÖNGIN·LOBESAN·
HAT·DIE·ASCH·EHRLICH·BSTATTEN·LAN

Martin Bucer travelled from Strasbourg to England in 1549 and was welcomed as a Protestant refugee. He taught at Cambridge University and was a consultant to Thomas Cranmer on the wording of the second Book of Common Prayer, published in 1552.

In 1525 in Zurich the mass was abolished and replaced by a simpler communion service, conducted from a wooden table rather than a stone altar. Places of worship changed too. Walls were whitewashed, windows were furnished with plain glass, and pews were simple benches. Much of what would happen in England in the 1540s had already happened in Zurich.

The other significant figure in the European Reformation was John Calvin (1509–64), although he was of a later generation and his influence was less direct on events in England. Exiled from his native France, Calvin found refuge in Geneva in 1536 and, after a brief period in Strasbourg, returned to Geneva and devoted the rest of his life to the

French Protestant John Calvin (1509–64) is best known for expounding the doctrine of predestination. He influenced refugees who fled England during Mary's reign and returned under Elizabeth.

reform of its church. He was in favour of a ministry of pastors, doctors and elders and saw Christianity as a godly civic community, not the individual encounter with God that the Lollards had believed in. Calvin is most associated with the doctrine of predestination, which originated in passages of St Paul's letters that described those who were saved as elected. Predestination envisaged that God had chosen those who were to be saved, and the remainder had to contend with the consequence of their sins. It answered the conundrum of why some listeners responded to hearing the gospel while others remained unmoved.

Calvin is important because he was a prolific writer and preacher and trained missionaries to export his reforms, especially throughout France. By the 1560s Calvinism had become an international movement, influential in all areas of Europe that were not Lutheran. Although Calvinism influenced the Elizabethan church in England, it is arguable that it had a greater impact in Scotland, where it helped launch Presbyterianism, and later in Wales, where it inspired the dominant form of chapel worship, Calvinistic Methodism.

Scripture was at the heart of Renaissance humanism and of Protestant doctrine. To truly understand religion, it was logical that the Bible had more authority than interpretations found in church art and book illustrations. Erasmus wanted to see the Bible translated into every vernacular tongue. This was the great project in the years immediately preceding the English Reformation. England was by no means the first country to have a Bible printed in its native language.

Several editions in German were published in the fifteenth century and there was a Czech Bible published in 1488.

Illegal English Bibles had existed since the Lollards had translated it in the 1390s, but they were circulated in manuscript form and touched relatively few people. Printed works such as the Latin *Biblia Pauperum*, or 'Poor Man's Bible', had offered a condensed version of the Bible, with illustrations, but concentrated on Bible stories at the expense of Bible teaching. If people had access to the Bible in their own tongue, it had the potential to make priests of everyone, but that was a contentious issue. To more conservative biblical scholars such as Thomas More and John Fisher, Bishop of Rochester, an English Bible would be intolerable because it would undermine theological authority and would lead people into error. That is why the first New Testament printed in English was published in Worms in the Rhineland of Germany, not in England.

William Tyndale (*c.* 1494–1536) devoted his life to the translation of the Bible into English. But, to complete his work, he had to leave England, since none of the reform-minded clergymen who had been inspired by Erasmus,

The laity learned much of their religion from pictures, such as this painting at Walsoken (Norfolk) of the well-known Bible story of the Slaughter of the Innocents ordered by King Herod. Reformers argued that pictures were a poor substitute for Bible reading.

The invention of the printing press vastly increased the supply of religious literature to lay folk. The *Biblia Pauperum* ('Poor Man's Bible') was a book illustrated with Bible stories. This image shows the Resurrection, flanked by Old Testament stories of Samson and Jonah.

notably Bishop Cuthbert Tunstall of London, would support him. Tyndale, like Erasmus, based his translations on Greek and Hebrew texts and therefore provided a more accurate rendition of the Bible than the standard Vulgate. His New Testament was published in 1525–6, followed by sections of the Old Testament from 1529, and was distributed on the black market. Dissemination into England via the North Sea ports was significant enough for the authorities to raid merchant ships, stationers and booksellers, seizing and burning the copies they could impound, and infiltrating cells of Bible readers to confiscate their copies. A few of the readers who were caught were tried for heresy, reflecting the hard line taken after Sir Thomas More succeeded Cardinal Wolsey as Lord Chancellor in 1529. One of them was James Bainham, of the Middle Temple in London, who defied his accusers by saying that 'the truth of holy Scripture was never, these eight hundred years past, so plainly and expressly declared'. He was burned at the stake in 1532.

Tyndale never enjoyed the fruits of his labours. Henry VIII wanted him extradited to England – Tyndale opposed the annulment of Henry's first marriage – but the imperial authorities in the Duchy of Brabant tried him for heresy after he was lured from his hiding place in Antwerp and taken to Vilvoorde near Brussels. He was convicted of heresy and died by strangulation, after which his body was burned, making him one of the first of the great Protestant martyrs. Tyndale should be better known than he is. His work marks the beginning of the golden age of the English language. Many of the phrases that he translated into English – 'salt of the earth', 'give up the ghost' and 'fight the good fight' – show his gift for expressive language and have been absorbed into common speech.

William Tyndale was responsible for the first printed English New Testament. Tyndale lived and worked largely in exile.

Tyndale was condemned to death by strangulation in Brussels in 1536. He is said to have called out on the scaffold, 'Open the King of England's eyes'. Two years later the King ordered an English Bible to be placed in every parish church.

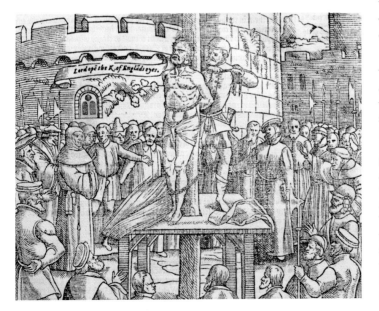

Lord ope the K. of Englãdis eyes.

THE BREAK WITH ROME

SUCCESSION IN THE Tudor dynasty would prove to be the catalyst of great changes in religion. Henry VII, who reigned from 1485 to 1509, had wished to establish a dynastic alliance with the ruling house of Spain and so in 1501 his eldest son, Arthur, was married to Katherine of Aragon (1485–1536), daughter of Ferdinand, King of Spain. Five months later, Arthur died. It was agreed that Katherine should marry Arthur's younger brother, Henry, but the marriage took place only after a great deal of diplomatic manoeuvring and after Pope Julius II granted a special dispensation, by which time Henry had already been crowned King.

The only child of Henry and Katherine to survive to adulthood was Mary, born in 1516. For Henry VIII this was a crisis – the prospect that his only daughter would marry a foreign prince and that England would become the overseas dependency of a foreign kingdom. Having apparently proved his fertility with at least two mistresses, Henry came to regard his marriage to Katherine as cursed. Visits to pray at the shrine of Our Lady of Walsingham had been of no benefit. The solution to his troubles appeared to be found in an injunction in the Old Testament Book of Leviticus that warns that 'if a man shall take his brother's wife, it is an unclean thing'. It seemed they were destined to remain without a son. By the mid-1520s, when Katherine was in her forties, his attention was diverted to Anne Boleyn (1501–36), more than a decade younger than his wife.

Henry needed to extricate himself from his unholy union and charged his chief minister, the Lord Chancellor Cardinal Thomas Wolsey (1470–1530), with fixing it. Wolsey had to persuade the Pope that Henry's marriage had never been lawful and should be annulled. (He was not asking for a divorce, since that would have implied that the marriage was legitimate in the first place.) The issue was politically sensitive because Katherine's nephew, Charles V, the Habsburg Holy Roman Emperor, was the dominant figure in European political affairs. Pope Clement VII was mindful of this, and was in any case disinclined to overturn the decision

Katherine of Aragon, in a miniature painted c.1525. Her brief marriage to Prince Arthur in 1501, which she said was unconsummated, was used by Henry to argue that his marriage to her was invalid.

Henry VIII's second wife, Anne Boleyn, was an educated woman and came from a family with strong reformist views, but she fell from favour and was executed in 1536 on a charge of adultery.

of his predecessor. Eventually, in 1529, Wolsey convened an ecclesiastical court in London, with the papal legate, Cardinal Campeggio, in attendance, at which Katherine was forced to plead publicly with the King. She claimed that her marriage to Arthur had never been consummated and had therefore been no marriage at all (the couple were fifteen when they married and her husband was dead before he was sixteen). But the Pope deferred making a decision, effectively thwarting Henry's ambition. Cardinal Wolsey was dismissed, ostensibly for fraud and corruption, and died within the year on his way to imprisonment in the Tower of London.

The idea that an annulment could proceed without the approval of the Pope had not crossed Henry's mind. Anne Boleyn was said to have introduced the King to William Tyndale's book *On the Obedience of a Christian Man and How Christian Rulers Ought to Govern* (1528). It promoted the idea that a king should be head of the church as well as of the state. Scholars examined ancient sources and concluded that the King had once been head of the church in England but had been usurped by the Pope. Frustrated by papal procrastination, Henry came round to the idea that he should act unilaterally. He had the English church declare his union with Katherine null and void and married Anne Boleyn in 1533 in Westminster Abbey.

If Henry's quarrel with the Pope was simply about his wife, then the church would have remained Catholic but under different leadership. But Henry sympathised with many of the criticisms of the church, was broadly in favour of an English Bible and seems to have lost faith in pilgrimage, relics and shrines.

Thomas Wolsey, painted c. 1520 wearing the scarlet robes of a cardinal. He was made responsible for negotiating the annulment of Henry VIII's marriage to Katherine of Aragon.

Henry VIII, in a portrait of 1537 by Hans Holbein the Younger. By this time Henry had established the King's authority over the church in England, had executed his second wife, and was in the process of dissolving the monasteries.

He also had grievances over the legal and financial workings of the church. In 1530 he issued writs first against the Archbishop of Canterbury and then the church as a whole. These were writs of praemunire, or 'lesser treason', on the basis that the church had infringed the King's law by the existence of its own courts. A fine of £100,000 was paid, but Henry wanted more. Parliament was encouraged to criticise the church on familiar

Sir Thomas More, seen here in a portrait by Hans Holbein the Younger, was Lord Chancellor from 1529 to 1532. He opposed the break with Rome and refused to acknowledge Henry as Supreme Head of the Church of England.

grounds – its unholy wealth, its worldly clergy and the like – and Henry reminded the bishops and abbots that swearing an allegiance to Rome, to where taxes were payable, made him question where their chief loyalties lay.

Inevitably there were traditionalists who opposed the changes that Henry was intending to make. Katherine of Aragon was backed publicly by John Fisher, Bishop of Rochester, and privately by Henry's Chancellor, Thomas More. Both of them opposed the King's efforts to become head of the church, as did William Warham, Archbishop of Canterbury. Conveniently for Henry, Warham died in 1532. The Pope arguably made matters worse by elevating Fisher to the status of cardinal. Both More and Fisher were tried for heresy and executed.

Behind Henry's changes to the church were important advisors. Anne Boleyn was an intelligent and educated evangelical who was more than just a love interest. Thomas Cromwell (1485–1540) was the brilliant politician who piloted the necessary legislation through Parliament that culminated with the passing of the Act of Supremacy in 1534. The legislation merged spiritual and secular power in the person of the monarch and ended the Pope's authority over the church in England. As Supreme Head of the Church, Henry was now able to investigate and discipline clergy himself, and to supervise religious doctrine and the liturgy. In practice, these powers were vested in Thomas Cromwell, acting as the King's Vicar-General.

The third influential figure who came to the fore at this time was Thomas Cranmer (1489–1556). Cranmer was consecrated as Archbishop of Canterbury in 1533. The choice was a surprising one because he had not previously held high clerical office. Since 1527 he had been employed to canvass support among Europe's theologians for Henry's annulment. He witnessed the ongoing Reformation first-hand in Switzerland, Strasbourg, and in Nuremburg, where he married a German woman, Margarete, setting aside his vow of celibacy. This, however, had to be kept secret when he became Archbishop, but he was chosen for the role because of his Protestant leanings, and because the Boleyn family lobbied on his behalf. He would survive Anne Boleyn's fall from grace, and became instrumental in liturgical reform under Edward VI.

Cromwell turned his attention to religious houses that owed allegiance, and taxes, to Rome. The monastic orders were international institutions, swearing allegiance to the Pope, and so were especially vulnerable. Monasticism was in long-term decline, since almost all religious houses experienced falling recruitment in the later Middle Ages. Some smaller, undermanned houses were amalgamated, or even closed down so that their endowments could be put to better uses. In Cambridge, for example, Jesus College in 1496 inherited the estates of a closed nunnery. In the end the dissolution of the monasteries came to look like the greedy expropriation of church property (such as was underway in German cities), but it did not begin that way.

One of the implications of the Act of Supremacy was that taxes owed

Thomas Cromwell was Henry VIII's chief minister from 1532 to 1540. He orchestrated the Act of Supremacy, the dissolution of the monasteries and Henry's marriage to Anne Boleyn. His downfall came after he arranged Henry's disastrous fourth marriage to Anne of Cleves.

EARL OF ESSEX.

to Rome were now payable to the king. In 1535 Thomas Cromwell initiated a census and audit of the nation's religious institutions, known as the *Valor Ecclesiasticus*, which would allow an accurate assessment of taxes payable. Attention was naturally focused on the most Roman of institutions, the monasteries. Moreover, many (not all) were wealthy, indeed richer than the profligate Henry VIII, who had spent much of the wealth accrued by his father on a lavish lifestyle and gestures, of which the Field of the Cloth of Gold, his

extravagantly staged meeting with the King of France in 1520, was the pinnacle. The King knew how rich the monasteries were. Only in 1522, for example, the Abbot of Glastonbury had been able to loan him £1,000.

The tax assessment was followed swiftly by a visitation of the monasteries in 1535 and 1536. Its commissioners were instructed to remain alert to superstitious practices, phoney relics promoted for fraudulent purposes, deference to Rome, and any evidence that men and women were failing to live

The parish church of St Mary in Bungay (Suffolk) was shared with a nunnery, which was suppressed in 1536 and now stands ruinous at the east end of the church.

Deerhurst Priory (Gloucestershire) became a parish church at the dissolution, while the associated domestic ranges are incorporated into the farmhouse, on the right side of the picture.

these places, such as Lanercost (Cumbria), Abbey Dore (Herefordshire) and Malmesbury (Wiltshire), the scale and quality of monastic architecture would be appreciated for many centuries to come. The cloisters and domestic buildings almost invariably vanished, however. There are a few notable exceptions, such as Forde (Dorset), Beaulieu (Hampshire) and Coombe (Warwickshire), where the domestic buildings were adapted for use by their new owners.

The abbey at Coombe (Warwickshire) was converted to a country house, as shown here in a seventeenth-century engraving.

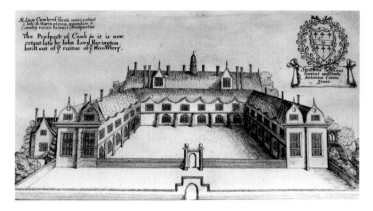

Most monasteries, which had once been alive with prayer and were busy places at the heart of communities, were suddenly deserted and silent. Their dissolution had a marked impact on many towns and cities. Shrewsbury lost a monastery and three friaries. Canterbury lost three monastic communities and three friaries. In many places masonry and furniture were scavenged from the ruins, and timber was broken up for firewood. Such practices ensured that the monasteries could never again be revived. It was officially sanctioned vandalism. Many of the spoils of monastic plundering have come to be precious works of art. The magnificent choir stalls and misericords made for Whalley Abbey (Lancashire) in the second decade of the fifteenth century were removed to the parish church.

Buildwas Abbey (Shropshire), as viewed c. 1790 by Edward Dayes. 250 years after they were abandoned, many monasteries had become picturesque ruins.

The person who gained most from the dissolution of the monasteries was the King. Evangelicals had wanted the wealth of the monasteries diverted into charitable and educational enterprises, but their hopes went unfulfilled. Monastic estates and their treasures passed to the crown, administered by the

The tower is all that survives of the former Evesham Abbey (Worcester-shire), the site of which is now a public park.

Court of Augmentations, but land was soon sold off to ensure political support and to strengthen the King's finances.

The level of popular support for the dissolution of the monasteries is difficult to ascertain, but there were plenty of places where their closure was opposed. Traditionalists may have been encouraged by the fall of Anne Boleyn in 1536,

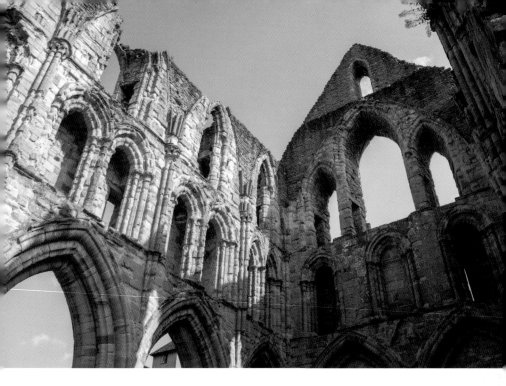

which may have given momentum to the protests later in the year. Resentment against the closure of monasteries and disquiet about the trend of other reforming policies fuelled unrest that began in Lincolnshire in October 1536. The Lincolnshire Rising was soon followed by a larger protest known as the Pilgrimage of Grace. These protestors marched behind the banner of the Five Wounds of Christ. Their quarrel was not with Henry VIII, since they considered that loyalty to traditional religion did not mean disloyalty to the King, but with men such as Cromwell and Cranmer who were driving religious policy.

The Pilgrimage of Grace gathered such momentum that by December 1536 over thirty thousand people are thought to have joined the march towards London. Their demands were simple. They wanted the return of the old ways, prosecution of heretics, the reinstatement of Mary as the legitimate heir to the throne, and the restoration of the monasteries. Henry drew their anger by sending the Duke of Norfolk to meet them. In a placatory mood, he agreed to their demands,

Wenlock Priory (Shropshire) was founded by Mercian kings in the seventh century but was re-established after the Norman Conquest as a Cluniac priory. It was dissolved in 1540. The best-preserved parts of the abbey church are the transepts.

The ruined gatehouse is all that survives of St Benet's Abbey on the Norfolk Broads. The windmill was built inside it in the eighteenth century.

The ruined gatehouse of Cleeve Abbey (Somerset), dissolved in 1537. One of its monks, John Hooper, would later become Bishop of Gloucester and was burned at the stake in 1555.

The ruins of Rievaulx Abbey (North Yorkshire), painted by John Wootton in 1728. The estate was owned by the Duncombe family, seen here in the foreground, while labourers work on the repair of the ruins.

bar restoration of the monasteries. But nothing happened. Mary continued to be known as 'the Lady Mary', and over two hundred of the pilgrims were executed, including Robert Aske, leader of the Yorkshire contingent.

The Protestant faction was in the ascendant, but only for the short term. Henry VIII lost three wives in less than three years. Katherine of Aragon died in 1536 and Anne Boleyn was executed later the same year. Jane Seymour died after childbirth in 1538. Thomas Cromwell tried to broker a fourth marriage with a princess from Protestant Germany, but made the mistake of picking Anne of Cleves, who, in Henry's eyes, was not as pretty as her picture. It was the beginning of the end for Cromwell. Cranmer negotiated his way through these difficulties but there were conservative bishops to counterbalance his influence with the King. And what the Pilgrimage of Grace told him, if Henry cared to listen, was that England was becoming a divided nation.

THE
BYBLE IN
ENGLYSHE

REFORM IN THE PARISHES

ONE OF THE grievances that motivated the Pilgrimage of Grace was with a move to curtail traditional religious practices in the parishes, namely the 1536 Act for the Abrogation of Certain Holydays. Festivals could no longer be held during harvest time, between 1 July and 29 September. The initial reason for curtailing the traditional festive calendar was that many saints' days fell during the busiest period of the agricultural year, which was said to encourage laziness among the labouring classes. Soon, however, there was talk of 'superstitious and childish observances', a conflation of idleness with idolatry. For example, the feast of St Nicholas and the Holy Innocents, when boys dressed up as priests and bishops and performed mock rituals (the world turned upside down, of which the pantomime dame is the modern descendant), was banned in 1541 as an affront to ecclesiastical dignity. It is just one example of how the religious and cultural life of the parish changed from the 1530s.

The first doctrinal statement of the newly created Church of England was the Ten Articles of 1536. In these, the King was to be acknowledged as head of the church (praying for the Pope was dropped from the liturgy), and his children by Anne Boleyn were to be the legitimate heirs. What was most noticed, however, was the effect on parish worship. Only three sacraments were mentioned, baptism, penance and the Eucharist. Veneration of images and intercession for the dead were allowed, but in a qualified form, in an attempt to

The title page of the Great Bible, over nine thousand copies of which were printed by 1541. The title page emphasises the authority of the King over the clergy and the people.

curb superstitious excesses. Pilgrimage was discouraged, on the basis that men would please God more by carrying out their daily business and providing for their families. In 1537 *The Institution of a Christian Man*, popularly known as the *Bishops' Book*, was published to explain to the priesthood the implications of the Ten Articles. The *Bishops' Book* reflects the delicate balance of conservative and reformist sympathisers among the senior clergy and in this respect was a compromise document. It reinstated some of the sacraments – matrimony, ordination and extreme unction – but it was ambiguous about transubstantiation and stressed the importance of scripture and Luther's doctrine of justification by faith.

Henry did not like the *Bishops' Book*, but the one piece of reforming legislation that he fully supported was the publication of an English Bible. William Tyndale had made himself *persona non grata* for opposing the annulment of Henry's marriage to Katherine. Nevertheless his New Testament and his translation of Old Testament books were supplemented by further translations by Miles Coverdale that, although not based on Hebrew texts, closely followed Martin Luther's translation. They made up the 'Great Bible', which in 1538, by royal injunction, was ordered to be purchased and displayed in every parish church by the following Easter. That the majority of the population was illiterate was beside the point – there were people to read aloud for those who could not read it themselves.

In the late 1530s reformist bishops, including Archbishop Cranmer, Nicholas Shaxton, Bishop of Salisbury, and Hugh Latimer, elevated to the see of Worcester in 1535, were able to implement some key reforms. Latimer preached against many components of traditional devotion. He disliked the cult of the saints, and images with supposed miraculous powers, such as the image of the Virgin Mary at Walsingham. There were too many candles in parish churches and too much emphasis on purgatory. So in 1538 Thomas Cromwell issued an injunction against some traditional practices, stressing that the people should not put trust in practices not authenticated in scripture. The kinds of thing he had in mind were 'wandering to pilgrimages, offering of money, candles or tapers to images or relics, or kissing or licking the same', all of which were acts of idolatry and superstition. It provoked the first wave of outright iconoclasm in English parish churches. Major shrines were closed down and their images and relics were taken to Cromwell in London. Statues of Our Lady were brought from Walsingham, Worcester, Caversham, Ipswich and Penrhys in South Wales. Thomas Becket was proclaimed a traitor and his shrine in Canterbury Cathedral was stripped and the bones burned.

The destruction of some of these shrines, coupled with the ongoing closure of the monasteries and confiscation of their relics, reduced the opportunity to seek intercession from the saints. Destruction was occasionally a public event.

Bishop Hugh Latimer came to prominence as a preacher in the 1520s, advocating publication of an English Bible. He was Bishop of Worcester between 1535 and 1539, when he resigned over the Six Articles.

The rood from Boxley Abbey in Kent was confiscated and paraded to show how strings were used to manipulate the figure of Christ, exposing the fraud of the monks. It was burned publicly in London. So was a famous image from Llandderfel in North Wales, burned in Smithfield, where it was used to roast alive a Franciscan friar, John Forest, who refused to renounce the Pope. On the same night, the rood from St Margaret Pattens church in the City of London was broken up 'by certeine lewd persons, Fleminges and Englishe men, and some persons of the said parishe'. These were clearly not mass

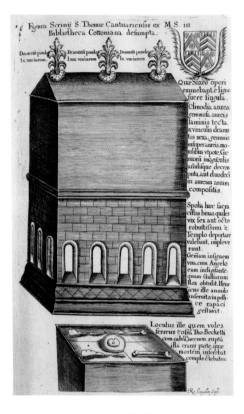

Figura Scrinij S.Thomæ Cantuariensis ex M.S. in Bibliotheca Cottoniana desumpta.

Deauratii pondo lx. vnciarum.   Deauratii pondo lxxx. vnciarum.   Deauratii pondo lx. vnciarum.

Quæ Saxeo operi eminebant,e ligno fuere singula. Clinodia aurea gemmosa,aureis laminis tecta, & vinculis deaura tis nexa,gemmis insuper aureis,mo nilibus vtpote,Ge monii insigniculis aureisque decem pula,aut duodeci in auream aream compositis.

Spolia hæc sacra cistas binas quales vix sex aut octo robustißimi è Templo deportare valebant, impleve runt. Gemmam insignem vna,cum Angelo eam indigitante, quam Galliarum Rex obtulit,Henr icus ille annulo inseruit;in polli ce rapaci gestauit.

Loculus ille,quem vides ferreum ossa Tho.Becketti cum calvâ,necnon rupta illa cranij parte,quæ mortem interchat comple ctebatur.

The shrine of St Thomas Becket in Canterbury Cathedral was destroyed in 1538. This seventeenth-century reconstruction of it was based on images in medieval manuscripts.

uprisings but the zeal of a minority. In other places there was local resistance. At Chilham in Kent the image of the rood was adorned with silver shoes, which was just the sort of extravagant folly that reformers wanted to eradicate, but, although the shoes were removed, the rood itself remained and was valid as long as it was not abused.

The pace of reform was checked by the fall of Thomas Cromwell, who was executed in 1540 as a traitor and heretic, after traditionalists persuaded Henry that Cromwell's extreme view of the Eucharist was opposed to that of the King. But it was also checked by the reservations of the King. In 1539 the Act of Six Articles was passed. Its chief clause was a victory for traditionalists because it reinforced belief in transubstantiation, denial of which was heresy. Bishops Shaxton and Latimer both resigned. The conservative bishops were led by Stephen Gardiner, Bishop of Winchester, who subsequently persuaded Henry that unrestricted access to the English Bible had been a mistake. Henry was said to have complained that the word of God was 'disputed, rhymed, sung and jangled in every ale house and tavern'. From 1543 noblemen and gentlewomen might read the Bible in private, but reading of it in public, or by 'women … artificers, prentices, journeymen, serving men of the degrees of yeomen or under, husbandmen or labourers' was forbidden.

Henry had not liked the *Bishops' Book* because it took him further than he wanted to go. So in 1543 it was replaced by *A Necessary Doctrine and Erudition for Any Christian Man*, popularly known as the *King's Book*. In it the doctrine of justification by faith alone was dropped, and good works arising from faith were considered to be a valid path to salvation. This must have meant little to most Christians, but they would have noticed other changes. In 1544 and 1545 came English-language liturgies and prayers, which the King ordered to be used in every parish church. The result was a brand of English Catholicism without the Pope.

The impact of these reforms across the country was uneven. Chester's first bishop, John Bird, complained that his diocese was backward-looking and clung to traditional ways. In Kent, by contrast, Archbishop Cranmer was able to promote into influential positions churchmen of a reforming tendency. One of them was Nicholas Ridley (*c.* 1500–55), who was made chaplain at the cathedral, then vicar of Herne in Kent, before elevation to the sees of Rochester and then London. Traditional practices and refusal to conform to the new procedures, such as the use of English where prescribed, were attacked in diocesan visitations, while radical priests refused to issue candles or conduct rituals such as covering images at Lent. Traditional practices continued even in Cranmer's diocese, however. John Cros was able in 1542 to go to the church of Milton near Canterbury and set a garland of flowers on the image of St Margaret and say mass there. An attempt to destroy the rood at Chilham in 1543 was resisted by the parishioners by reference to the *King's Book*. In other parishes radicalism was found among the parishioners rather than the clergy, some of whom reported their priests for setting up images. The attack on purgatory saw a decline in prayers for all but the recent dead, and guilds and fraternities suffered a decline. Collegiate churches that provided teams of priests to act as a community of intercession also declined. The parish of Warwick St Mary surrendered its college to the crown and bought back the assets, simultaneously acquiring the grant of a school and a town charter.

Nicholas Ridley became Bishop of Rochester in 1547 and Bishop of London in 1550. He was partly responsible for depriving Stephen Gardiner and Edmund Bonner of their sees in 1550, but Gardiner and Bonner would have their revenge in Mary's reign.

In the 1530s half of England's population was under twenty, a generation much more receptive to modern ideas, with less to forget, and quicker to adopt anti-authoritarian sentiment than older generations. One of these young people was Henry's heir, Edward, born to his third wife, Jane Seymour, in 1538. Unlike the previous generation, Edward had been tutored by reformers and had no loyalty to the old ways. Although the cause of reform had been tempered by the conservative leanings of the King, Henry did nothing to prevent a Protestant education for his son, perhaps fearing that a more conservative upbringing might have opened the door again to the Pope.

Edward succeeded to the throne in 1547. During his reign the realm was governed by a Regency Council, headed at first by his uncle Edward Seymour, Duke of Somerset, who enjoyed the title Protector of the Realm. Under his leadership the reformers were in control and the pace of reform accelerated. Rebellion at home in 1549, the cause of which was partly about religious reform, saw the Protector ousted, to be replaced by John Dudley, Duke of Northumberland, but reform continued. With Archbishop Thomas Cranmer firmly on the side of reform, many of the conservative bishops lost their sees during Edward's reign. The loudest critics of the Edwardian regime, Bishops Gardiner of Winchester and Bonner of London, were imprisoned. Norwich, Durham, Gloucester and Chichester all had new bishops, among whom the rising star was Nicholas Ridley, who replaced Bonner as Bishop of London in 1550.

This painting, produced in the 1560s, shows Henry VIII on his deathbed, pointing towards his successor, Edward VI. To the right of Edward are members of his council, including the Protector of the Realm, the Duke of Somerset, and John Dudley, Duke of Northumberland. Below Edward, the Pope is crushed by 'the worde of the Lord'.

Fotheringhay church (Northamptonshire) was built in the fifteenth century as a collegiate church. After the Reformation it continued as a parish church, but the chancel of the medieval building, which stood on the left side of the picture, was considered surplus to requirements and was pulled down.

In Edward's reign influential reformers were among the Protestant refugees who fled the Catholic Counter-Reformation in Europe. London had its own church for refugees, known as the Strangers' Church, housed in an old Austin friary, which was given to them by the government in 1550 (it was destroyed in the Blitz in 1940). Its superintendent was the Polish reformer Jan Laski. Other reformers included Martin Bucer from Strasbourg and Peter Martyr from Italy, both of whom obtained important university posts. It had the effect of exposing England to the more radical Protestant ideas in Europe, and took England beyond the influence of Luther.

One of the problems of the Henrician Reformation, especially for theologians, had been that it was encumbered by the King's eccentricities. Henry's theology was stranded between the loss of purgatory and the denial of justification by faith, a state of affairs that could not continue. The ambiguities of Henry's position had at least managed to accommodate a wide range of opinions, but theologically they were contradictory.

Moves by the new regime were cautious at first. Among the first pieces of legislation to be introduced was the abolition of the Six Articles, the official statement of belief during Henry's reign. It was followed by the Chantries Act. Once the notion of purgatory was rejected, institutions that said masses for the dead became superfluous. The Act expressly stated that it was intended to end the 'phantasising vain opinions of purgatory' and its associated masses. Like the monasteries, these institutions were financed by endowments that reformers thought could be put to much better use. In practice the Chantries Act also affected collegiate churches, almshouses and hospitals, in all of which prayers and masses were said for the souls of their founders, in addition to their various charitable works. Humanist reformers, such as the London merchant Henry Brinkelow, wanted the wealth of chantries to be diverted for 'the use of the Commonwealth, and unto the provision of the poor according to the doctrine of scripture'. In practice these high ideals were rarely fulfilled,

The parish church of Crediton (Devon), viewed from the south. The long chancel, to the right of the tower, indicates that it was once a collegiate church. The chapter house is at the right-hand end. The college had provided a school, which was replaced by a grammar school by a charter of 1560.

During Edward VI's reign the figures in this reredos at St Cuthbert's church in Wells (Somerset) were removed. The structure was plastered over but was revealed again during restoration of the church in the nineteenth century.

At Binham Priory (Norfolk) the rood-screen figures were concealed by whitewash and replaced by text from the Great Bible.

and the wealth of chantries disappeared mainly into the government's coffers. One of the unintended consequences of the Chantries Act was the further depletion of the priesthood. Many chantry priests, often former monks, had acted as auxiliary priests in the parish church but now they were pensioned off.

A more thorough cleansing of the old church than had been achieved under Henry was set in train. The new policy was issued by a series of Injunctions, and enforced by visitation. Now the effect of the Reformation was to be felt in every parish church. The images that were once 'the books of unlearned men' were to be discarded. Parishes were ordered to 'destroy all shrines, covering of shrines … paintings and all other monuments of feigned miracles, pilgrimages, idolatry and superstition so that there remain no memory of the same in walls, windows or elsewhere'. The order to remove stained-glass images was extreme, as there was never any evidence that people knelt before them in veneration. Parishes did not have the resources to replace window glass and there is no evidence that it was carried out, Westminster Abbey being a high-profile exception. Wall-paintings were whitewashed over, inadvertently preserving them for Victorian and later restorers to discover. In some places there was sufficient public enthusiasm to initiate spontaneous destruction of images.

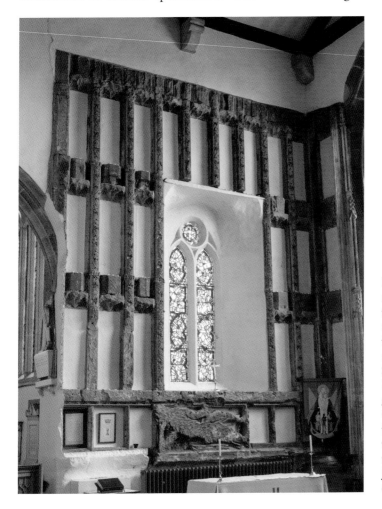

Figures were removed from this now-damaged fifteenth-century reredos at Wells St Cuthbert. It showed the genealogy of Christ in the form of a tree, with as its root the figure of Jesse, father of King David.

Norfolk has many rood screens on which images of saints were defaced during the Reformation, simply by scraping away the paint. At Barton Turf the face of the Pope, on the left, has been deliberately disfigured.

Outside St Paul's Cathedral, from the open-air pulpit at Paul's Cross, Bishop William Barlow ridiculed a collection of cult images that were subsequently smashed up by local boys. In Norwich, several enthusiasts, including one parish priest, tore down and removed images from the city's numerous parish churches. The city authorities could do little to stop it. The official visitation also made a spectacle of its iconoclasm. In Shropshire a bonfire of saints' bones was made at Much

The rood screen at North Burlingham (Norfolk) was installed as late as 1536. A little more than a decade later the faces of the saints, including St Withburga, were deliberately scraped away.

These mutilated faces of Saints Augustine and Gregory are on the rood-screen doors at Foxley (Norfolk).

Above:
At Ringland
(Norfolk) the
hands and faces
of Saints Andrew
and Peter have
been scraped off
the wood.

Above right: The
defaced figure of
the East Anglian
saint Etheldreda,
portrayed as
an abbess, is at
Horsham St Faith
(Norfolk).

Wenlock and in Shrewsbury images from the town's parish churches were burned in the market place.

Injunctions forbade the burning of candles, with the exception of two candles before the altar. It meant that rood lights had to be extinguished. The lighting of candles had made the rood seem like a devotional image, so after the lights were removed many roods were taken down. Nearly all those in London churches were destroyed, with little recorded opposition, although one of the figures on the rood in St Paul's Cathedral fell and killed a workman.

Other changes affected parish life. Processions were outlawed, and bells were rung only before the sermon, silencing the sanctus bell that was traditionally rung during the Elevation of the Host at mass. There were no more private holy days for bakers, smiths and the like, and use of holy water or candles in the cleansing of sin or exorcism of demons was ended. The laity were encouraged to bequeath money to the poor box, rather than to the traditional 'pardons, pilgrimages, trentals [the saying of thirty requiem masses], decking of images, offering of candles, giving to friars and upon other like blind devotions'. Money bequeathed for the purchase of 'torches, lights, tapers and lamps' was also to be diverted to the poor. Evidence from wills shows that bequests to chantries and guilds were already declining during the sixteenth century, at the expense of a rise in donations to charities and the poor. This could be interpreted as a declining allegiance to traditional ways or as realisation that change was coming. Festivals such as Corpus Christi and Plough Monday

Below left: The painted figure of St Laurence on the rood-screen base at Widecombe in the Moor (Devon) has been defaced.

This bench-end at Abbotsham (Devon) shows the crucified Christ with the chipped-off faces of St John and the Virgin Mary.

St George,
seen here on
the screen at
Wellingham
(Norfolk), was
one of the few
saints to have
survived the
Reformation.
He has been
England's
patron saint
since Edward III
promoted his
cult in the 1340s.

wakes were suppressed. Candles were prohibited from Candlemas (the festival of the Purification of the Virgin Mary and the Presentation of Christ in the Temple, originally 14 February), ashes from Ash Wednesday, and palms from Palm Sunday. In a short space of time the drama, movement and spectacle of the traditional church had been suppressed. The theatrical power of the old liturgy had gone.

In a few places there was open insurrection. In 1548 William Body, Archdeacon of Cornwall, was murdered while active in the Lizard peninsula removing images from churches. Near Scarborough, a chantry commissioner, Matthew White, and his wife were among those abducted from their beds by night and murdered on the moors above Seamer. But these were exceptional cases. Elsewhere, little defiance of the visitation is recorded. Local studies of the Reformation years portray a mixed reaction to the changes under Edward. Some parishes were quicker to shed the trappings of traditional religion than others. The parish of St Laurence in Reading stripped the church of its images in 1547 and sold off the rood and the church plate used in the mass for £60. By contrast, at Winterslow in rural Wiltshire the parish did not remove images from the church until a year later, and was quick to reinstate its traditional Easter and May Day celebrations when the chance arose in 1553.

Removing the trappings of traditional religion made way for the building of a new way of worship. In the first year of

Edward's reign a series of injunctions and Acts of Parliament brought a marked increase in the use of English in the liturgy of the parish church. All Christians were encouraged to read the Great Bible, the 'special food of man's soul', and parishes were ordered to acquire a copy of the *Paraphrases* on the Gospels, written by Erasmus. Every parish was required to provide a sermon at least four times a year and, in parishes where the

The rood screen at Attleborough (Norfolk) was repainted with heraldic devices in the seventeenth century.

The 'Golgotha' at Cullompton (Devon) is a unique survival. This oak base is carved with skulls and stones and was originally fixed above the rood screen. Mortices for the rood and supporting figures can still be seen.

priest was unable to preach himself, he could read aloud from a *Book of Homilies* that explained the Protestant reforms, some of which were written by Archbishop Cranmer himself. For now, the mass was said in Latin, but the readings from the Bible (the Epistle and the Gospel) were read in English.

The most radical shift to the Protestant form of worship came in 1549 when use of the new Book of Common Prayer was enshrined in an Act of Uniformity. English was now the sole language of worship. Many theologians and senior clergy had by now rejected transubstantiation, as advocated by Luther, in favour of the more radical interpretation of Zwingli – that the Eucharist was a commemoration of the Last Supper in which bread and wine remained as just bread and wine. The Book of Common Prayer, written by Archbishop Cranmer, included a new communion service, subtitled 'the supper of the Lord and Holy Communion, commonly called the mass'. Evangelicals hated the word 'mass', but its use effectively allowed Christians to read into the new communion service what they wanted to. It was a shrewd way of placating the conservatives, although the emphasis of the service had changed decisively. Elevating the consecrated elements, with its overtones of a sacrificial offering, was discontinued, and the text made clear that the communion was an act of thanksgiving. The structure of the communion service may have retained some of the character of the old Catholic mass, but no communicant could fail to notice the radical shift from Latin to English. Christians would no longer worship in a sacred language, but in the common tongue. Some churches in London were already doing this, but in other parts of the country there was less enthusiasm. In 1549 there was a rebellion in south-west England, the 'Prayer-Book Rebellion', which resented the ritual impoverishment of the new way of worship, and the use of the vernacular (in a region where for some people the language of everyday speech was Cornish). The rebels laid siege to Exeter and demanded a return to the

Latin liturgy. Although the rebellion was quelled, it contributed to the downfall of the Duke of Somerset.

The pulpit was central to the dissemination of Protestant ideas, but it could also be used to promote doctrine that was not approved by the church authorities. For that reason it was controlled by government. Under Henry VIII and at the beginning of Edward's reign parish priests had been obliged to preach quarterly, but this was curtailed in 1548. Only licensed preachers were allowed to operate, so that seditious and contentious preachers were suppressed, and debate on particularly controversial issues, such as the real presence of Christ in the Eucharist, was prevented.

The other important innovation of these years was the legalisation in 1549 of clerical marriage. Marriage also ceased to be a sacrament, which meant that it was no longer indissoluble.

Archbishop Thomas Cranmer, in a portrait by Gerlache Flicke of 1545–6. Cranmer was the author of the *Book of Common Prayer*.

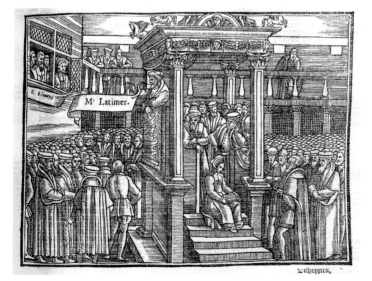

Bishop Latimer preaching in the Privy Garden in the Palace of Whitehall, from a pulpit established there by Henry VIII. Outdoor preaching was common in the Reformation years.

Stone altars were removed in 1550, reinstated in Mary's reign and removed again under Elizabeth. This rare survival at Farmcote (Gloucestershire) is placed on top of a wooden communion table, a curious amalgamation of once mutually exclusive fixtures.

On this bench-end of the 1540s at Milverton (Somerset) is an asperge, a holy-water vessel and sprinkler used to sprinkle consecrated water over the altar, part of the ritual equipment sold off after mass was abolished.

Divorce therefore became legal. Many clergy married (and some soon obtained a divorce), some merely formalising a previously informal and discreet relationship, others simply to assert their Protestant credentials. The one prominent churchman who had been married for sixteen years already was of course the Archbishop of Canterbury, who could now legally and openly abandon his double life.

When Nicholas Ridley was made Bishop of Rochester in 1547 he began ordering the removal of stone altars, which had connotations of sacrifice. They were replaced by wooden communion tables, placed so as to be more visible to the congregation and to emphasise the commemorative nature of the Eucharist. Other bishops were also overseeing their removal by the time a formal order for their replacement came in late 1550. Another contentious issue was clerical vestments. John Hooper had infamously protested against vestments for his ordination in 1551 as Bishop of Gloucester, although he was eventually persuaded to conform. Since the other trappings of the mass had been abolished, it was logical that the cope and vestment worn by the priest to celebrate mass should also be abolished. In 1552 the priest celebrating communion was required to wear only a plain surplice.

Both Martin Bucer and Peter Martyr were consulted over the revised Book of Common Prayer published in 1552. It made significant changes to the order of service for the Eucharist, including the abolition of the old vestments mentioned above. Communicants were still required to kneel, which provoked a debate that was resolved only when it was made clear that kneeling did not imply adoration. However, it was the new form of words that upset the traditionalists. The sacrament was administered with the words 'Take and eat this, in remembrance that Christ died for thee, and feed on him in thy heart by faith, with thanksgiving'. The influence of the European reformers was clear. Christ was received not by bread in the mouth, but by faith in the heart. Mass had been abolished.

Edward VI allowed his council to increase the pace of religious reform, but the course of the Reformation took an unexpected turn after the young King's death in 1553.

MARY AND ELIZABETH

T HE PROTESTANT CHURCH was still a work in progress when the King fell terminally ill in 1553. To block the inevitable accession of Mary, the dying Edward VI and his advisors tried to make Lady Jane Grey (1537–54) the legitimate heir, since she was the great-granddaughter of Henry VII through his younger daughter, Mary, and was a Protestant. Her reign lasted only nine days. Mary enjoyed popular support as the daughter of Henry VIII and Katherine of Aragon, and she quickly assumed the throne. Mary was staunchly Catholic and married her second cousin, the future Philip II of Spain, in 1554. Leading churchmen now suffered a reversal of fortunes, especially those who had plotted on behalf of Jane Grey. Archbishop Cranmer and Bishops Latimer, Hooper and Ridley were arrested for treason. Imprisoned bishops Stephen Gardiner and Edmund Bonner were released and assumed their former bishoprics of Winchester and London respectively. Mary's reign is sometimes known as the Marian Reformation, because it was not simply a backward-looking restoration of everything from the old religion, although it was marked by the return of the Catholic mass and obedience to Rome. Cardinal Reginald Pole, who had been in exile since 1532 when he refused to accept Henry VIII's second marriage and refused to acknowledge the Act of Supremacy, was appointed Papal Legate to England on Mary's accession, and in 1556 he replaced Cranmer as Archbishop of Canterbury. He was effectively chief minister during Mary's reign.

The execution on Guernsey in 1556 of Katherine Cawches, her daughters Guillemine Gilbert and Perrotine Massey, and an infant grandson, was described by John Foxe as 'a tragical, lamentable, and most pitiful history, full of most cruel and tyrannical murder'.

Mary I oversaw a partial return to traditional religion, but burning heretics at the stake sealed her reputation as Bloody Mary.

Radical Protestants were driven underground, worshipping in secret, or sought refuge abroad in Protestant strongholds, where many of them were further radicalised. Exiles in Geneva produced a new Bible translation, known as the Geneva Bible. Other Protestants convinced themselves that it was acceptable to attend Catholic rituals. They became known as Nicodemites, named after the Jewish leader Nicodemus, who consulted Christ under cover of darkness. Some more open Protestants were scathing about them, especially since those Protestants who were exposed by the authorities and refused to confess the error of their ways were burned at the stake. Not for nothing would the Queen become known as Bloody Mary, although largely because Protestant sufferings were documented by John Foxe, who published the first edition of his *Actes and Monuments*, popularly known as the *Book of Martyrs*, in 1563. It has proved to be one of the most influential works of propaganda published in English. England's antipathy to the Roman Catholic Church was forged by the events of these years, catalogued in Foxe's remarkable book.

John Foxe (1516–87) in a woodcut dated 1587. His *Book of Martyrs* was one of the most powerful works of Protestant propaganda.

Cardinal Reginald Pole returned from self-imposed exile in 1553 and was Archbishop of Canterbury from 1556. He died from influenza on the same day as Queen Mary in 1558.

The burning of Protestants would prove a disaster for the reputation of Mary and the Roman Catholic Church. It served to rehabilitate the senior clergy who had schemed on behalf of Lady Jane Grey. Bishops Latimer, Ridley and Hooper were burned at the stake. Cranmer was tortured into confession of his errors and signed recantations of his Protestant beliefs. Repentance did not bring clemency, however, and he was scheduled to be burned in March 1556. In a carefully orchestrated showpiece before his execution, he was made to attend the University Church in Oxford, where he was expected to confess his sins in public. Instead, he confounded his tormentors by retracting his confessions and denouncing the Pope as Antichrist before he was pulled from the pulpit by angry friars.

Many of the martyrs described by Foxe were common folk. The family of William Mount, a farmer from Much Bentley in Essex, shunned the parish church and joined a

Bishops Latimer and Ridley were burned at the stake together in Oxford in 1556.

Thomas Cranmer plucked from the pulpit in the University Church, Oxford, before his execution in 1556. He was expected to confess his sins, but retracted his earlier confession instead.

When he was burnt at the stake, Cranmer wanted the hand that had signed his false confessions to be purged first.

Above: 'Seven Godly and constant martyrs', who had denied the Catholic mass, burned at Smithfield in January 1556. They included Thomas Whittle, a married priest, and Bartlet Green, who had studied under Peter Martyr at Oxford.

Below: Dr Rowland Taylor was burned at the stake in Hadleigh (Suffolk) in February 1556. He had preached against popish corruption but, according to John Foxe, was betrayed by a 'mammonist' and 'whoremonger'.

group dedicated to Bible reading and prayer, but they were betrayed by the parish priest, a reminder perhaps that local scores were being settled in these years. Ten members of the group were burned at Colchester in 1555. William, his wife Alice and their maid Rose were bound together 'and were joyfully tied to the stakes, calling on God and exhorting the people earnestly to flee from idolatry'. Christopher Waide, a linen weaver, and Margery Polley, a widow, both withstood the intimidating inquisition of the Bishop of Rochester and went to their deaths singing psalms.

The Marian regime could not reverse all of the changes made since the 1530s. The monasteries could never be brought back as their assets and revenues had been seized by the crown, and the abbey churches were in ruins. Chantry lands had been sold off, often to sitting tenants, and their priests had left the ministry. Changes were therefore concentrated upon restoring the Catholic liturgy in the parishes.

The hated Bishop Bonner of London was often portrayed as a sadist in John Foxe's *Book of Martyrs*, either burning the hands of his victims or scourging them.

When Catholicism was restored under Mary, the parishioners of Ludham (Norfolk) replaced the great rood that had been destroyed in the previous decade with a tympanum painted with the Crucifixion, the Virgin Mary and St John.

Much of the paraphernalia of Christian worship that had been discarded in the previous years was now reinstated. In many places items had been concealed in the time of Edward VI, and these altars, vestments, images and roods were taken from their hiding places and put back where the parish thought they belonged. Other parishes had to sell their communion tables and raise money from donations to buy back the equipment they needed. Edmund Bonner initiated a visitation of his London diocese in 1554 and called for all churches to re-equip with items that were sold after the mass was abolished in 1552. These included books, a chalice and cover (or paten), a pyx (a silver receptacle for the reserved sacrament), a pax (a small tablet depicting the Crucifixion that was kissed by the congregation at mass), a sanctus bell, vestments for the priests, hangings for the altar, processional cross, censer and candlesticks. In 1557 a visitation of Canterbury diocese found that many parishes failed to acquire

everything they needed until the new order was enforced. Many people welcomed these changes, but Lawrence Saunders, of the supposedly Protestant parish of All Hallows Bread Street in London, complained that the parish restored the mass even before the government had legislated for it. In Yorkshire, Robert Parkyn rejoiced that 'altars were re-edified, pictures or images set up' and that 'all the English service of late used was voluntarily laid away and the Latin taken up again'. In this respect the Marian church was successful. In other ways it could not restore the old liturgy. The campaigns against purgatory and prayers for the dead had largely prevailed, and previous confiscations of their assets made people wary of investing in new guilds and chantries. In general, then, the high altar of the parish church was restored under Mary, but not the side altars. Marian Catholicism had a narrower devotional range than the pre-Reformation church.

Elizabeth I assumed the throne after Mary's untimely death in 1558. Her forty-five year reign was a period of greater stability, during which the Church of England, with the monarch as Supreme Governor, was firmly established.

Mary died in November 1558. She had no heir and so the crown passed to her younger half-sister Elizabeth, daughter of Anne Boleyn. Elizabeth was a Protestant, albeit a conservative one, and was twenty-five years old and unmarried. Her prospects of a match with one of the royal houses of Europe looked unpromising if she was not prepared to commit herself to Catholicism, and so the long-term future of the national church was far less certain than it seems in hindsight.

A sixteenth-century woodcut by John Daye shows communicants kneeling around the altar table to receive Holy Communion, in a ceremony that had been stripped of its mystical trappings.

Elizabeth oversaw a religious settlement that became the foundation of the Anglican Church. She is credited with moderating some of the more radical Protestants and made some concessions to traditionalists – it is said that but for her England's cathedrals would have gone the same way as its monasteries. The Act of Supremacy of 1559 settled the constitutional relationship between church and monarch, and from this time the monarch has been known as the Supreme Governor of the Church of England. The form of worship was dealt with in an Act of Uniformity, and was based on the 1552 Book of Common Prayer, with some revisions. The most significant concerned the order of service for the Eucharist. The new version retained the Protestant ideology, in stressing that the communion was offered 'in remembrance of Christ', but satisfied some of the traditionalists with the added phrase: 'the Body of our Lord Jesus Christ, which was given for thee, preserve thy body and soul unto everlasting life.' The Act also enforced attendance at church, on pain of a fine payable to the poor box.

None of the bishops who had been appointed under Mary voted for the Act of Uniformity and there was a clear-out at the highest levels of the church, bringing in a new Protestant Archbishop of Canterbury, Matthew Parker, and men such as Edwin Sandys, who had escaped from Marshalsea prison and lived in exile during Mary's reign, and who was appointed Bishop of Worcester in 1559. Only about three hundred

In the chancel at Langley Chapel (Shropshire) the communion table is set forward and has benches around it. (The table is a replica made after the original was stolen in 1969.)

At Deerhurst (Gloucestershire) the seventeenth-century arrangement of the chancel, with seating behind the communion table, is a rare survival.

members of the lower clergy resigned or were deprived of office, and the church could ill afford to lose them, as it had a generally depleted and demoralised priesthood. Not until the 1570s did a new generation of men trained at Protestant universities replace the older generation that had served through the Reformation.

The plain interior of Langley Chapel (Shropshire), with whitewashed walls and simple pews, demonstrates the preference for simplicity of the church interior.

Injunctions were issued to remove items of the old religion that had reappeared in Mary's reign, with renewed instructions to set up a new communion table. A determined effort was made to rid churches of these objects once and for all, in order 'to plant true religion' without the possibility of ever again returning to the old ways. Churchwardens of every parish were required to make inventories of vestments, plate and books, and compliance was enforced by visitation. Where evidence was found that objects were being hidden away, the culprits were often harshly treated. Nine parishioners of Aysgarth in North Yorkshire were forced in 1567 into a humiliating public confession and were then required to burn the offending objects in public. Churchwardens' accounts from across the country document compliance with the new laws, but not with any great enthusiasm. Rood-loft timbers and stone altars were removed, many of them ending up as domestic building materials, just as old copes were adapted as bed hangings.

The early reforms of the reign were interim measures in advance of the definitive statement of the doctrinal beliefs of the English church. These were the Thirty-Nine Articles, issued in 1563 and reiterated in 1571. They represented the Anglican compromise between Catholics and Protestants in the church and Parliament, but there were many people on the edges who could not accept it. Preaching remained a licensed activity and a new *Book of Homilies* was issued that could be read out in lieu of a sermon. Under the influence of Calvin, some churchmen rejected the notion of a priesthood and all its trappings, including their 'Romish rags' – in 1566 thirty-seven London clergy were suspended for refusing to wear vestments, a list that included the author John Foxe.

By the end of the century England was effectively multi-denominational. The most ardent Protestants were nicknamed puritans, and some of them had broken away and formed their own independent congregations, the beginning of the Congregationalist denomination. Until 1581 Catholics

This painted board of the Ten Commandments at Ludlow (Shropshire) is dated 1561. It is flanked by the sacred monogram of Christ's name and a lily representing the Virgin Mary.

The Ten Commandments are painted on the walls at Cameley (Somerset), replacing the medieval wall-paintings. Texts were commonly painted on walls after the Reformation.

could openly refuse to attend church services. Thereafter they worshipped in secret, especially in traditional strongholds such as Lancashire. It was essentially backward-looking, because England was cut off from Catholic developments in mainland Europe. Establishment of a college in Douai to train Catholic missionaries demonstrated that the Roman Catholic Church had not given up on England, however.

By the 1570s the English Reformation had gone as far as it was going to. The parish churches had changed immeasurably over the previous forty years. There was a sharp decline in church-building, although repairs had to be undertaken where necessary, and the prevailing Gothic style was as yet unchallenged by the Renaissance in architecture. Churches had much plainer interiors, although that should not be interpreted as anti-art. To begin with, the images in medieval churches were not art for art's sake, and plainness and simplicity are in themselves a form of aesthetic expression. Benches were installed in many parish churches in the

Royal arms had been placed in churches since the Act of Supremacy in 1534, signifying that the King was Supreme Head of the Church. This example at Westerham (Kent) is the only survivor from Edward VI's reign.

The Marian rood at Ludham (Norfolk) was soon reversed and the arms of Elizabeth I were painted and filled the chancel arch above the screen.

ANNo 1574

GOD raue the queen

The royal arms at Beckington (Somerset) are dated 1574, during the reign of Elizabeth I, and are among the oldest surviving royal arms in an English church.

Elizabethan period and remained medieval in character. The communion table had replaced the stone altar. Whitewashed walls were adorned with texts from scripture, either directly on plaster or on boards. Many rood screens remained standing, although bereft of the medieval rood and shorn of their medieval significance. Above the screen, where the rood had stood, were now the royal arms. Royal arms had been introduced to churches in the reign of Henry VIII and were a constant reminder that the Reformation was enacted by the King himself. Early examples were removed during Mary's reign. Many survive from Elizabeth's reign, although most examples from that period were later replaced, and most of the surviving royal arms in parish churches belong to the Georgian period.

The pulpit and the poor box were not new, but only a minority of churches had either of them in the sixteenth century. Not until the early seventeenth century, under

James I, did pulpits become an essential requirement of Anglican worship, which is why so many medieval churches have pulpits of that date. The pulpit was to be the focus of Anglican worship until the nineteenth century. Old rood screens were useful because they screened off the chancel, which had lost its former importance.

The artists and craftsmen who had been commissioned to produce religious works now found employment on

At the Reformation the rood was taken down from Parracombe old church (Devon) but the screen remained. Above it, in the eighteenth century, a wooden tympanum was erected on which were painted the royal arms, Ten Commandments, Apostles' Creed and Lord's Prayer.

The pulpit remained a platform for both radicals and traditionalists in the sixteenth century. This Elizabethan pulpit is at Monksilver (Somerset).

The poor box became a common addition to parish churches after the Reformation, but most examples, like this one at Ash Priors (Somerset), belong to the seventeenth century and later.

secular subjects. This is well illustrated in the career of the most famous painter of the period, Hans Holbein the Younger (1497–1543). He began his career painting altarpieces and ended it painting kings. Sculptors found increasing employment designing tombs for the nobility, where Renaissance art first flourished in England. Just as money that was once spent endowing chantries was now spent on monuments, wealthy benefactors who once funded church-building now invested their money in secular projects, mainly their own homes. It is the beginning of the era of the country house.

The Act of Union between England and Wales had been passed in 1536. It meant that Wales experienced the Reformation just as England did. There was a Welsh Bible and Prayer Book, which proved just as important for the flourishing of the native language as their English counterparts. Although the Anglican Church was the

Craftsmen who had worked on religious subjects now found secular commissions. The tomb of the Elizabethan statesman William Cecil (1520–98) at Stamford St Martin (Lincolnshire) is in the Renaissance style.

best represented denomination in Wales into the twentieth century, in the eighteenth century a Welsh reformation of sorts began with the rise of the predominant nonconformist denomination, Calvinistic Methodism.

Attempts to export the English Reformation to Ireland were unsuccessful. It was a colonial as much as a religious enterprise and for that reason was fiercely resisted. Henry VIII had made Ireland a subordinate kingdom of England and in areas under effective English control its monasteries were dissolved along with those of England. But the Reformation, with its emphasis on everyday language, was conducted in English from the English-speaking Dublin Pale – there was no Gaelic New Testament until 1603. Catholic missionaries trained on the Continent were active in Ireland and were more effective than Protestant preachers, many of whom were Englishmen who had failed to advance their careers in England. It is from this period that in Ireland Catholicism became synonymous with nationalism.

Scotland had its own Reformation. Celebration of the mass and allegiance to the Pope were abolished in 1560, but there was no royal supremacy. The liturgy in Scotland was the Book of Common Order, written by John Knox and influenced by Calvin. By the end of the sixteenth century Scotland had adopted its own radical structure, with regional presbyteries made up of local Kirk sessions of pastors, elders and deacons, all of them answerable to a General Assembly.

The response of the Roman Catholic Church to the radical reforms in parts of northern Europe is known as the Counter-Reformation. The Council of Trent (Trento in northern Italy) was in session from 1545 to 1563. It condemned the Protestant heretics, and reaffirmed traditional doctrine, including transubstantiation, veneration of saints, use of the Vulgate Bible, and the unwritten traditions of the church. Church discipline was addressed, however – something that had been easy for the Protestant radicals to criticise – and the education of priests was improved. This was aided by new religious orders, the most influential of which was the Society of Jesus, whose members are known as Jesuits, founded by a Basque former soldier, Ignatius Loyola, in 1540. The Jesuits became the chief missionaries of the Roman Catholic Church, in the Protestant countries of Europe and further afield.

The Church of England was not reconciled to its Catholic past until the nineteenth century. Legal and social impediments to Roman Catholic worship were removed in 1829. Discovery and publication of medieval liturgies, combined with an appetite for a more spiritual form of worship and of church architecture, restored a more Catholic form of worship in the Church of England. Use of the archaic English of the Book of Common Prayer (which had been revised in 1662) and the King James Bible of 1611 went some way to restoring a sacred language, just as Latin had been in the Middle Ages. In the second half of the nineteenth century, the interior appearance of churches changed markedly again. Prominence was given to the chancel instead of the pulpit, stone altars were reintroduced, and there was a revival in the applied arts such as stained glass, as well as reversion to more elaborate priestly vestments and altar hangings. Texts on walls went out of favour and, in places, wall-paintings replaced them.

Amends have been made for some of the Reformation's more destructive acts. Walsingham (Norfolk) has again become a destination for pilgrims and a new statue of Our Lady was set up there in 1922. In 1909, at a ceremony attended by the Prince and Princess of Wales, the deeds to the ruins of Glastonbury Abbey were formally passed to the Archbishop of Canterbury. Glastonbury has now become a centre of pilgrimage for both Catholics and Anglicans, and the Reformation has been reinterpreted as part of the continuum of Christian worship in England.

FURTHER READING

Aston, Margaret. *England's Iconoclasts: Laws against Images*. Clarendon Press, 1988.

Bernard, G .W. *The King's Reformation: Henry VIII and the Remaking of the English Church*. Yale University Press, 2005.

Collinson, Patrick. *The Reformation*. Phoenix, 2005.

Daniell, David. *William Tyndale: a Biography*. Yale University Press, 2001.

Duffy, Eamon. *The Stripping of the Altars: Traditional Religion in England c. 1400–1580*. Yale University Press, 1992.

Duffy, Eamon. *The Voices of Morebath: Reformation and Rebellion in an English Village*. Yale University Press, 2001.

Duffy, Eamon. *Saints, Sacrilege and Sedition: Religion and Conflict in the Tudor Reformations*. Bloomsbury Continuum, 2014.

Ives, Eric. *The Reformation Experience: Living through the Turbulent Sixteenth Century*. Lion Hudson, 2012.

Loades, David (editor). *John Foxe and the English Reformation*. Scolar Press, 1997.

MacCulloch, Diarmaid. *Thomas Cranmer: a Life*. Yale University Press, 1996.

MacCulloch, Diarmaid. *Tudor Church Militant: Edward VI and the Protestant Reformation*. Allen Lane, 1999.

MacCulloch, Diarmaid. *The Later Reformation in England, 1547–1603*. Palgrave Macmillan, 2001.

MacCulloch, Diarmaid. *Reformation: Europe's House Divided*. Penguin, 2004.

Marshall, Peter. *Reformation England, 1480–1642*. Bloomsbury, second edition 2012.

Rex, Richard. *Henry VIII and the English Reformation*. Palgrave Macmillan, 2006.

Ryrie, Alec. *The Age of Reformation: the Tudor and Stuart Realms 1485–1603*. Pearson Educational, 2009.

PLACES TO VISIT

THE REFORMATION WAS a period of loss, when more physical items were taken from churches than were created for them. Some of the art works removed from churches during the Reformation found their way into museums. The Victoria and Albert Museum, Cromwell Road, London SW7 2RL, has collections that include sculpted images, fragments of screens, and the paraphernalia of pre-Reformation worship.

The most conspicuous casualties of the Reformation were the monasteries, many of which have been preserved in their ruined state and are open to the public. These can be found across the country, but any selective list would have to include Glastonbury Abbey (Somerset), Netley Abbey (Hampshire),

The altarpiece now at Thornham Parva (Suffolk) was made in the 1330s for Thetford Priory. Painted on wood panels, it is a rare surviving work of art from the once rich heritage of English monasticism.

Castle Acre Priory (Norfolk) is one of many ruined monasteries now in the care of the state, recognising the rich and important heritage of Catholic England.

The seating in the chancel at Hailes (Gloucestershire) is arranged around the former position of the communion table, which was intended to demystify the rite of Holy Communion.

Rievaulx Abbey, Whitby Abbey, Fountains Abbey and Byland Abbey (all North Yorkshire). Other monasteries were taken over as parish churches or were elevated to cathedral status. Examples where the whole monastic church has survived include Westminster Abbey, Gloucester Cathedral, Bristol Cathedral, Peterborough Cathedral, Chester Cathedral, Tewkesbury Abbey (Gloucestershire), Christchurch Priory, Sherborne Abbey (both Dorset), Bath Abbey, Dunster Priory, Stogursey Priory (all Somerset), Romsey Abbey (Hampshire), Cartmel Priory (Cumbria) and Dorchester Abbey (Oxfordshire). In most places only a portion of the abbey church has survived, and among these the finest examples include Great Malvern Priory (Worcestershire), Malmesbury Abbey (Wiltshire), Boxgrove Priory (West Sussex), Worksop Priory (Nottinghamshire), Brinkburn Priory and Hexham Priory (Northumberland), Binham Priory (Norfolk), Abbey Dore (Herefordshire), Waltham Abbey (Essex), Lanercost Priory and St Bees Priory (Cumbria) and St Germans Priory (Cornwall).

There are several places where evidence of the iconoclasm of the Reformation years can be seen. At Cullompton (Devon) the base of the rood, known as the Golgotha, has survived but is no longer placed on the screen. In Wells St Cuthbert (Somerset) there are two stone reredoses belonging to side altars, the figures of which were removed. Among the numerous rood screens of East Anglia there are several in which the saints have been defaced or painted over, including Barton Turf, Horsham St Faith, North Burlingham, Binham Priory, Foxley and Ringland (all Norfolk).

Fewer churches retain the fittings and internal appearance of the Reformation, largely because of the Gothic Revival of the nineteenth century, when plainness was no longer acceptable. Early surviving royal arms are rare. At Rushbrooke (Suffolk) are the arms of Henry VIII, but whether they were made for the church or were brought there later is disputed. The only Edwardian example is at Westerham (Kent), but examples from the reign of Elizabeth include Hoo St Werburgh (Kent), Beckington (Somerset), Ludham, Tivetshall St Margaret (both Norfolk) and Preston (Suffolk). Preston also has Elizabethan painted inscriptions, as does Puddletown (Dorset). The liturgical arrangement of chancels, likewise anathema to the nineteenth-century revivalists, is also rare, but communion tables of the period are at Deerhurst and Hailes (both Gloucestershire, the latter now moved back against the east wall), and at Langley Chapel (Shropshire), which also retains its plain pews from the refitting of the church in the 1560s.

INDEX